Cooking Tools

By Inez Snyder

Children's Press®
A Division of Scholastic Inc.
New York / Toronto / London / Auckland / Sydney
Mexico City / New Delhi / Hong Kong
Danbury, Connecticut

Photo Credits: Cover and all photos by Maura B. McConnell
Contributing Editor: Jennifer Silate
Book Design: Daniel Hosek

Library of Congress Cataloging-in-Publication Data

Snyder, Inez.
Cooking tools / by Inez Snyder.
     p. cm. -- (Tools)
Includes bibliographical references and index.
Summary: A boy and his father make pancakes for breakfast, using the appropriate kitchen utensils.
   ISBN 0-516-23977-5 (lib.) - ISBN 0-516-24035-8 (pbk.)
   1. Kitchen utensils--Juvenile literature [1. Kitchen utensils   2. Cookery] I. Title
   II. Series

TX656.S65 2002
641.5'028--dc21

                                                            2002001404

Contents

My name is Juan.

Dad and I are making pancakes for **breakfast**.

We will use many tools to cook.

5

These are **measuring cups**.

We will use them to **measure** the pancake mix and water.

I put one cup of mix in the bowl.

Dad pours the water into the bowl, too.

This is a **whisk**.

It is used to beat the mix and water together.

11

I use the whisk to beat the pancake **batter**.

13

It is time to cook
the pancakes.

Dad pours some batter
onto a hot pan.

This is a **spatula**.

A spatula is used to pick up food.

17

Dad uses the spatula to turn over the pancake.

Now, we will cook the other side.

19

The pancakes are done.

It is time to eat!

21

New Words

batter (**bat**-ur) a mixture thin enough to pour that becomes solid when cooked

breakfast (**brek**-fuhst) the first meal of the day

measure (**mezh**-ur) to find out the size or weight of something

measuring cups (**mezh**-ur-ing **kuhps**) cups that are used to measure food

spatula (**spach**-uh-luh) a tool with a broad, flat blade that bends easily; used to mix, spread, or lift food

whisk (**wisk**) a metal tool used for beating food

To Find Out More

Books

Kids Cook!
by Sarah Williamson and Zachary Williamson
Williamson Publishing

Mommy's Little Helper Cookbook
by Karen Brown
Simon & Schuster Children's

Web Site
Kids: Kings of the Kitchen
http://www.scoreone.com/kids_kitchen/
This Web site has lots of delicious recipes by kids from around the world.

Index

batter, 12, 14
breakfast, 4

pancake, 4,
  14, 18, 20

water, 6, 8, 10
whisk, 10, 12

measuring
  cups, 6

spatula, 16,
  18

About the Author

Inez Snyder writes and edits children's books. She also enjoys painting and cooking for her family.

Reading Consultants

Kris Flynn, Coordinator, Small School District Literacy, The San Diego County Office of Education

Shelly Forys, Certified Reading Recovery Specialist, W.J. Zahnow Elementary School, Waterloo, IL

Sue McAdams, Former President of the North Texas Reading Council of the IRA, and Early Literacy Consultant, Dallas, TX